EXTREME SCIENTISTS™

FOSSIL FINDERS:
PALEONTOLOGISTS

JUDY MONROE PETERSON

PowerKiDS press.
New York

To Elijah, Jonah, and Isabel

Published in 2009 by The Rosen Publishing Group, Inc.
29 East 21st Street, New York, NY 10010

First Edition

Editor: Amelie von Zumbusch
Book Design: Kate Laczynski
Photo Researcher: Jessica Gerweck

Photo Credits: Cover, pp. 1, 11 © Louie Psihoyos/Getty Images, Inc.; pp. 5, 9, 17, 19 © Getty Images, Inc.; pp. 7, 15 Shutterstock.com; p. 13 © AFP/Getty Images; p. 21 © National Geographic/Getty Images, Inc.

Library of Congress Cataloging-in-Publication Data

Peterson, Judy Monroe.
  Fossil finders : paleontologists / Judy Monroe Peterson. — 1st ed.
      p. cm. — (Extreme scientists)
  Includes index.
  ISBN 978-1-4042-4524-2 (library binding)
  1. Paleontologists—Juvenile literature. 2. Paleontology—Juvenile literature. 3. Dinosaurs—Juvenile literature. 4. Fossils—Juvenile literature. I. Title.
  QE714.7P57 2009
  560.92—dc22

                                        2008007150

Manufactured in the United States of America

CONTENTS

Learning About Ancient Life

Have you seen movies about dinosaurs? Scientists who study dinosaurs and other **ancient** life are called **paleontologists**. Paleontologists learn about early life by studying fossils. Fossils are the remains of plants and animals that are over 10,000 years old.

There are many kinds of fossils. Dinosaur bones and teeth are fossils. Ancient clamshells are fossils, too. There are also fossils of leaves, seeds, and wood. Some fossils are footprints! These fossils formed when mud in which dinosaurs and other ancient animals left footprints turned into rock. Animal trails can be fossils, too. Paleontologists have found trails of ancient worms in mud that became rock.

These paleontologists from the Field Museum, in Chicago, Illinois, are studying the bones of a dinosaur called a tyrannosaurus.

Finding Fossils

Just as there are many kinds of fossils, there are also many places to find fossils. People sometimes discover fossil shark teeth on seashores. Ancient bugs trapped in amber, or hardened tree sap, also have been known to wash up on seashores.

Other fossils are harder to find. Many fossils are deep in rocks. Paleontologists study where fossils were found in the past and then look for good sites to hunt for more fossils. A site is a place where ancient animals and plants once lived and left remains. Some sites where paleontologists have found fossils are old rocks, ice, and tar pits. Old mines, steep hillsides, and riverbeds are also good places to find fossils.

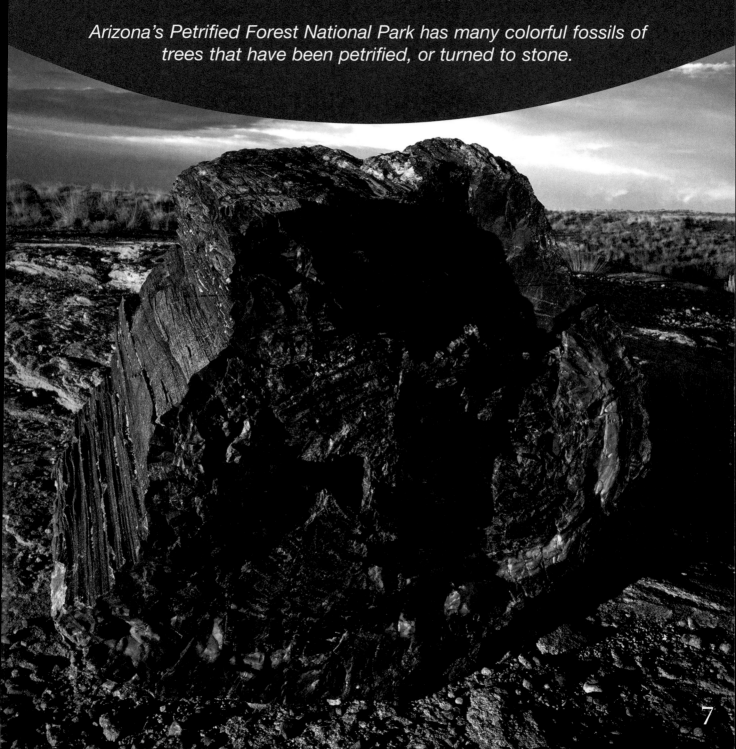

Arizona's Petrified Forest National Park has many colorful fossils of trees that have been petrified, or turned to stone.

Famous Fossil Sites

Good fossil sites are found all over the world. California's La Brea Tar Pits, Canada's Burgess shale, and Australia's Ediacara Hills are some well-known fossil sites. Another excellent site is Liaoning Province, in northeast China. About 130 million years ago, many animals and plants lived there. At the time, this land was warm and had many lakes.

So far, paleontologists have found the fossils of about 400 different animals and more than 60 different plants in Liaoning Province. Paleontologists have even discovered fossils of dinosaurs with small animals in their stomachs. They have dug up fossils of birds with plant seeds in their stomachs, too.

DID YOU KNOW?

Germany's Solnhofen limestone has fossils that are over 150 million years old. Paleontologists found fossils of an ancient bird called archaeopteryx there. This early bird had feathers and sharp teeth.

This fossil of a microraptor was found in Liaoning Province. Microraptors were small, birdlike dinosaurs with two pairs of wings.

Digging Up Fossils

Paleontologists dig in rock to uncover fossils. They work carefully. Fossils are fragile, or easy to break. Paleontologists remove tiny pieces of rock around fossils. They use tools such as hammers, saws, knives, and **chisels**. Little by little, the scientists free the fossils from the rock. Scientists use brushes to clear dirt away. Next, the fossils are covered in cloth or **plaster** to keep them safe.

Paleontologists keep records of where and how they found the fossils. They record this with maps, pictures, and movies. Paleontologists also measure and record each fossil's position and note how deep in the ground it was found. They store these facts in computers.

This paleontologist is using chisels, trowels, and brushes to dig up the fossil of a dinosaur called a protoceratops.

11

Cool Tools

Paleontologists unwrap fossils from a site in their labs. The scientists clean away dirt with **chemicals** or brushes. Then, the scientists use special tools to study the fossils. For example, paleontologists use X-ray machines and photography to measure the size and shape of fossils.

The scientists often use mass spectrometers to figure out how old fossils are. Mass spectrometers measure how much of certain isotopes, or forms, of one **element** are found in the rock around a fossil. This shows scientists how old these rocks, and the fossils in them, are.

DID YOU KNOW?

Paleontologists sometimes use clay or computers to make models of fossils. The scientists sometimes even put skin on models to see what animals once looked like.

Labs offer paleontologists a clean, safe place where they can study fossils closely for long periods of time.

Fossils Without Backbones

Most paleontologists study certain kinds of fossils. Some paleontologists study plant fossils. Others study animal fossils. Many paleontologists study invertebrates, or animals without backbones. Crabs, snails, worms, and ants are all invertebrates. Earth's first animals were invertebrates. Paleontologists have found fossils of invertebrates from 550 million years ago. Many fossils of invertebrates are found in rock called limestone.

When invertebrates die in water, their shells sometimes harden into fossils. Invertebrates covered by **sediment** can become fossils if the mud turns into rock. The shape of the invertebrate is pressed into the rock, forming a mold fossil. A mold sometimes fills with sediment that hardens and becomes a new fossil, called a cast.

Ammonite fossils, like these ones, are among the most common fossils. Ammonites lived in Earth's oceans over 60 million years ago.

Studying Dinosaurs

Some paleontologists study fossils of vertebrates, or animals with backbones. Dinosaurs were vertebrates. These ancient **reptiles** once lived around the world. They appeared about 230 million years ago, when Earth was very hot. Dinosaurs died out over 60 million years ago.

Some dinosaurs ate eggs, lizards, and turtles, but most dinosaurs ate plant leaves and fruit. Over time, some kinds of dinosaurs became huge because there was so much food to eat. Others dinosaurs became tall enough to reach leaves in treetops. Small, fast dinosaurs that hunted smaller animals also **evolved**.

DID YOU KNOW?

One of the largest dinosaurs was brachiosaurus. It was as tall as a four-story building and more than 90 feet (27 m) long. The smallest dinosaurs were as big as small birds.

Paleontologists in China found this tuojiangosaurus fossil. The tuojiangosaurus looked much like its North American relative, the stegosaurus.

Paleontologists also use fossils to study what Earth's land and **climate** were like long ago. They learn which animals and plants lived together. By studying fossils, paleontologists have discovered that Earth once looked much different than it does today.

When dinosaurs first appeared, Earth's land formed one huge **continent**. About 180 million years ago, this continent began to pull apart into pieces. As the pieces slowly moved, their average **temperature** and amount of rainfall changed. In the millions of years that followed, plants and animals in different places evolved differently.

DID YOU KNOW?

Nigersaurus, a 50-foot (15 m) dinosaur with 600 teeth, lived 110 million years ago in what is now Africa's Sahara desert. Then, the land was covered with rivers and forests.

This paleontologist is uncovering the fossil of a whale in San Juan Capistrano, California. The land there was once part of the ocean floor.

19

Discovering Early People

Paleontologists study fossils to learn how people changed over time and spread across Earth, too. They know that the earliest people appeared around 3 ½ million years ago in Africa. These people could stand, walk, and hold rocks and food in their hands.

About 100,000 years ago, fossils show that people changed. These people could make sharp rock tools, start fires for heat, and draw pictures. They began to move out of Africa. Fossils show that by 40,000 years ago, people in Africa, Asia, and Europe were like people today. They even buried their dead. In time, some of these people moved from Asia to Australia, North America, and South America.

These scientists are looking at the skull of an ancient person. The skull was found in Ileret, Kenya.

Becoming a Paleontologist

If you are interested in paleontology, you can visit **museums** to study fossils. There are summer camps at national forests that teach kids about dinosaurs and other fossils, too. You can also look for fossils in limestone along riverbanks, roads, and building sites. Dig out fossils with a hammer and chisel. At home, clean them with water and a toothbrush. Dry the fossils and paint them with glue to make them hard.

To become a paleontologist, you need to go to **college** and take classes in math, languages, and many branches of science. This knowledge will help you understand the clues about ancient life that fossils offer.

GLOSSARY

ancient (AYN-shent) Very old, from a long time ago.

chemicals (KEH-mih-kulz) Matter that can be mixed with other matter to cause changes.

chisels (CHIH-zulz) Sharp, metal tools.

climate (KLY-mit) The kind of weather a certain place has.

college (KO-lij) A school one can go to after high school.

continent (KON-tuh-nent) One of Earth's largest landmasses.

element (EH-luh-ment) The basic matter of which all things are made.

evolved (ih-VOLVD) Changed over many years.

museums (myoo-ZEE-umz) Places where art or historical pieces are safely kept for people to see and to study.

paleontologists (pay-lee-on-TAH-luh-jists) People who study things that lived in the past.

plaster (PLAS-ter) A mixture of sand, water, and lime that hardens as it dries.

reptiles (REP-tylz) Cold-blooded animals with plates called scales.

sediment (SEH-deh-ment) Rock, sand, or mud carried by wind or water.

temperature (TEM-pur-cher) How hot or cold something is.

WEB SITES

Due to the changing nature of Internet links, PowerKids Press has developed an online list of Web sites related to the subject of this book. This site is updated regularly. Please use this link to access the list:
www.powerkidslinks.com/exsci/paleo/